BIG CITY MANTRA

Bombshelter Press
Los Angeles

Cover Design: Josh Rose

Layout: Alan Berman

ISBN 0-941017-82-6

Big City Mantra is published by Bombshelter Press. Contributing authors are members of the Los Angeles Poets & Writers Collective, which sponsors writing workshops, readings, seminars, retreats, and literary publications including *ONTHEBUS*, *Wednesday*, and mo+th.

info@bombshelterpress.com

www.bombshelterpress.com

Los Angeles Poets & Writers Collective

www.jackgrapes.com

contents

Leslie Berliant

White Gold

A life without furniture is not half bad
although I had no idea I was walking into a monastic existence
complete with tatami mat and kokatsu table.
I fancy myself a daughter of the revolution
but really, I was a child pushed out onto
a suburban cul-de-sac'd street
where Mercedes and Volvos drove carefully
past rose bushes and lawns glowing a well-fertilized green.
Arrogance,
now there's a celebrity I'd like to snap in half
or perhaps keep close by as an antidote.
Regretting the purchase,
he wants to turn in the austerity for a house with rooms
with room enough
with obligations and gardeners and water bills.
I have never owned anything,
being a temporary sort of person.
Still, I am not unencumbered, it's a fragile balance.
"White gold or platinum?"
I laugh and say, "Don't tease me like that."

Alan Berman

The Show

A life without furniture is not half bad,
but I'm not counting—never was good at
fractions anyway. I have a bed, a chair,
and some mistakes that look like bags
full of marbles but lighter than oatmeal
and I still can't pick them up to get them
out of here. My neighbor's tv is mumbling
through the wall at me and I can't follow
the words, can only hear the falsely surprised athlete—
now there's a celebrity I'd like to snap in half—
no one can, though: he's too big.
I'd like to try, but only if there'd
be no reciprocity permitted. I'm like that:
prefer my disgusts to be single-lane,
no tolls. Life's maybe half as good as what
I would have expected by now, if I would have
even thought back then to expect anything
except loss. As it is, each day permits
a few blinks, some mumbling of my own,
and then recedes without comment.

Julia Soto Frazer

L.A. Hermit

A life without furniture is not half bad,
monkish swirls of nothing
charting the rooms, pots
of soup and slices of bread and
cheese and prayers
seven times a day, matins,
nones, something like that.

My vow of silence ended
with the remote control—
now there's a celebrity I'd like to snap in half
but it would be too easy
and big-lipped mean.
She's lifted and skinny and
halfway ascended,
dangling small feet, piñata
body hanging from klieg lights,
paparazzi flashing killer
bulbs up her skirt. Heaven
never looked so bright with
eyes closed, sitting on a zafu cushion.

Mari Weiss

Life Tartare

A life without furniture is not half bad.
It's been good on my back,
knowing I can throw it all in a suitcase and hail a cab.
No looking in the rearview. On to the next.

A life without email—PDA—GPS—cell is even better.
No electronic ankle cuff shackling me:
serving in-society detention to the self-important
knucklehead fuckwits who write the stupid rules.

A life without discernable talent is Ryan Seacrest.
Now there's a celebrity I'd like to snap in half,
chop into sound bite tartare and feed to the frenzied media.
May it stick in their gullets and no one know the Heimlich.

A life without satire is just too damn hard.
No frickin' fun. C'mon, you thin-skinned candy asses,
if life doesn't make you snort coffee out your nose sometimes
then pull over to the right and get outta my way.

I've got places to whee and things to gee while I spend
all my pennies in one fell swoop of inappropriate giggling
at appropriated ideals. I think I just wet myself.
Oh, hell, a life without life is just dead. Basically.

Vicki Whicker

Vail, Circa 1982

A life without furniture is not half bad
Ski bunny twenty-one
Full ski pass and benefits
Cocaine breakfast lunch and dinner
Hot pro mogul skier boyfriend
All good until the rich bitch pink minks start falling
Bunny slope lousy with Texas starlets
Proof poof of how nowhere I am
A shot of Cuervo, a shot of Jaeger, a shot of something on fire
Now there's a celebrity I'd like to snap in half
That other pro mogul super stud extraordinaire
Didn't win the contest today
Consolation bracket in my room or am I in his
With ski pants off and mirror on the table
And my god his thighs aren't soft
More like a Mack truck
Looking for a place to park
Boyfriend's on the podium
Scanning the room for a sunburned face
Silver trophy in his hands

Laura Caputo

Attitude

Muddled, furied, there is no sense of a hollow organ in this big brave soul.
Full from upstairs...buried somewhere below the surface, I have no more.
They said it would be easier.
They say you're a dragon, a triple dragon...a dragon with Fire.
You know what that means.
It means that I am good luck, good luck, good luck.
You know what it also means . . . some people just can't handle it . . . the fire part . . .
I burn so brightly, burn so much, burnout, perhaps.
This Chinese New Year's I will eat less, workout more, turn myself inside out and become a prairie dog by the time the end of the year comes.
I don't know what that means, what this means, what life means.
Fuck, fuck, fuck . . . not another word, "I don't want to hear another word out of your mouth," she says.
I can't believe it.
Who the hell does she think she is?
Telling me that words out of my mouth are unacceptable.
Well, what about if I think 'em, what about if I spell them with sign language.
Oh, yeah, I don't really know sign language . . . a few letters, but I think my hands would get tired from that.
You know what I'm going to do, mamma, I'm going to grow up and write a book about it . . . all the words you didn't want to hear come out of my mouth.
That's right, no I don't want you to know about it . . . I'll wait until you die to publish it. But I don't really want you to die . . .
Ah, back in the room . . . back to reality, or what they tell me is reality.
Did you know that last night I was chased my some bad men with guns . . .
well, actually I turned tail and went the other direction but I let my quote unquote friend get chased while I actually escaped.
I think they may have even raped her, and I did feel guilty but there was something about survival in that decision to run the other direction and let her get the punishment.
There are so many sides to this story that I haven't even begun to tell you about.
I mean seriously I could go on and on for days.
And that might be boring
for me, not for you . . .

Tim Giblin

Costa Rica, June 2006

>meanwhile, enjoy the journey. quit whinging about being alone. sometimes you are and sometimes
>you are not. each has its privileges. this is a spiritual experience you're on, pay attention to it.
>
>god bless.
>
>k
>From:
>Sent: Jun 7, 2006 5:45 PM
>To:
>Subject: Re: tim in costa rica
>
>thanks
>that was a good email, I might print it out and stick it in my bag, or I might tatoo it on my forehead..either way it was helpful, Im better now, I sold the van and took a boat to the mainland, and am heading towards the rainforest and panama.....I might call again when Im near a phone
>thank you
>tim

Mari Weiss

Linoleum Marker

"How do you like your gams and egg?"
I ask again for the umpteenth time.
Vacant stare is my only response.
Dumb silence drapes the walls,
burying any thought that might be my own.
My tongue has forgotten words
like *shower* and *fork* and *please.*
Mute gestures act as conversation
though most days pass without the attempt
and what do you say with two lines left to make the score?
If my mouth could recall laughter
would my ears recognize the sound?
Echoes of touch brush the back of my hand
and I am found in a memory
of somewhere other than this.
Clock chime brings me back,
faded linoleum marking the way,
and I am lost again in here.
I clear the dishes and my throat,
"I'll make tuna salad for lunch."

Josh Rose

United 93

How do you like your gam and egg?
Oh shhhhuuuuure, Mr. Goody Who's Your Doody?
I saw you hold your nose
I saw you shake your shaker
12:30 A.M.: United 93 is on. Do I:
A) Go to sleep a little early, lie there
Wishing I was wishier. Washier. Sleepier and such.
Or B) Stay upon it. Face the face of a movie that's really more
recreation than creation
and what do you say with two lines left to make the score?
In United 93, they say:
"Baby I swear, I promise, if I get out of this, I'm quitting tomorrow!
I quit tomorrow! I promise I'll quit tomorrow!"

I once thought about making a book of suicide notes
You know it would sell like gams and eggs
The problem I had was in how to procure them
not that it couldn't be done
It's just not a phone call I want to make
not just to Courtney Love, but anyone.
Death is still sacred. And that's why I pick A.

Shannon Murphy

Splitting a Headache

How do you like your gams and eggs?
Headless, featherless, boneless, split down the middle?
Cold, slack-fattied and temple-skinned, like an old-timer confined to an
        electric bed?
I know your kind, you slaughterhouse cheerleader, you keg-stood sideliner, you
calf-masseuse. You horse's ass.

Me and my skyscraper gams have cues to miss and cats to crack,
so snap to it and pop the yolk so we can get out of here already,
because this sourpatch mud will never taste sparrow enough, and godammit
I need something more today.
And what do you say with two lines left to make the score?

Last lines. Deadlines. Clumsy fools drop lines
like batons. With two lines left
I'd go fishing way up in another gam's mind. Pluck out a gaunt ruby guppie
from her Ganges, one that fed off of the corpse of an indigent grandmother
        and sucked whatever sicknesses out of her big toe long
after it mattered, after her heart stopped, after her pallbearers set her adrift
into a torrent of orphaned thoughts, of ordinary dirtiness, her last kiss before
the other girl's mind swallowed my reel.

What's with the Sunday-at-seven-am interrogation, stranger, and you asked
        for it so
cut that dumb gum-anvil guffaw and serve the damn eggs.

Alan Berman

Meal Time

How do you like your gams and egg?
No, that's not good. How about,
May I serve you some squeeze and crackers?
Probably too forward. Maybe,
I'm in the mood for a little straight shooting.
No, could be vague, misinterpreted.
Gotta be clear, dammit.
I'll get back to it. It's not easy,
this assignment. Say I get there with no prep?
And what *do* you say with two lines left to make the score?
Or what if there *is* no score, no one
to keep track? No one to announce
how well I'm doing?
Practice for the pets all I want
and I won't get far, except maybe with a
poodle or a ferret or a
recollection of attention
I had by accident,
by luck. I think I need
a new strategy.

Leslie Berliant

Open

How do you like your gams and egg?
A pretend sultry
come hither
tilt of her head.
Over easy, he said,
pushing her down on the bed
and laughing at her simplicity,
the simplicity of it all.
Words drowned in the cacophony of drugs, money and sex
and what do you say with two lines left to make the score?
Words are overrated, he thought
keeping track of orgasms,
his and hers.
What was the final count?
He went for sudden death,
with mad laughter and an even score.
She concentrated on his mouth,
the drip, drip, dripping yolks
of his thoughts, her heart like an open vein,
an open window, an open ending, a stop.

Tim Giblin

Colombia, August 2006

all in, no one dies for free
she smiles BLACK onto my
red coral contusions
walking distance
from a fat ingrown abscess
straddling guava corndogs
begging for latitude
cleaning my fingers
and sinking down to the bottom

Alan Berman

The Grid

Some fear dying. I fear never dying.
I practice every day just to make sure
I get it right, that it will come
on schedule. It's hard to read the grid
at this age: my eyes have other plans.
Based on my ID and birth date,
it looks as though I have only eleven weeks
left. But there are some uncertainties:
if I don't have the aneurysm, for instance.
I have a plan . . . at least part of one
that requires some assistance.
It has been true in my many hours
here with the other living
that, despite the grid, despite
intentions, independence is sacrificed
for the convenience of the system:
I need another who lives
to make the decision to jeopardize
her departure, so longed-for and
distant, to allow me to meet my due date.

Julia Soto Frazer

Home

Some fear dying. I fear never dying.
Brittle and phosphorescent, back to
where fish stand guard
and coral fingers suck, back to
my watery beginnings of caring monsters
and large-finned sea dragons, back to
the underwater prowl for dead things.

Sharks prefer not to kill, and their
eyeballs roll past me.

I have a plan . . . at least part of one:
plumped haven sand whip stinger
hidden green mystery lipstick—
a mimic, a cold-blooded fantasy
brood of stone flesh,
sticky with tar.

Drunk on caffeine, I lay awake with
tired words stretching like measuring tape and
couches cramming soft chenille and bagged
wooden hooves and big-screen TVs: it was
nothing like the ocean.

Leslie Berliant

Schrödinger's Cat

Some fear dying. I fear never dying.
I fear never feeling satisfied.
I fear still saying "I never had that"
when I'm 102.
There is a theory in physics
that a cat can be both dead and alive simultaneously
if it remains unobserved for long enough.
My ex used to try to explain it to me,
but, at the time, I could never really get it.
I have a plan . . . at least part of one.
How about we call it an either/or situation?
How about you make a choice, dead or alive?
Love or money?
Me or her?
Oh well, he never did like my ultimatums.
He only ever made one choice for me—
turns out it was the right one for him,
the wrong one for me.
But it did teach me how a person can be both dead and alive
all at the same time.

Vicki Whicker

A Part of One

Some fear dying, I fear never dying
I wish I could say that
Clearly I am one of the fearless
I want to live and live and live
Just so I can tell every generation
Relax this has been done before
Nothing is new under the sun
Global Cooling Global Warming
All been done before
I have a plan . . . at least part of one
Always a part of one
I dream of buying a house
I want my son to be in a house his mom owns
Just like I never dreamt of marriage for me
There are a lot of things I want for him
I plan to dream
Time is running out he is 14
Has smoked pot already
Has felt up a girl
And I am dying

Laura Caputo

The Partial Plan

Some fear dying. I fear never dying.
Hanging on forever, outliving everyone
Watching people come, people go
The buildings come and go
Happiness come and go
I'm on the upswing of happy
Hoping that it lasts longer than before
But expecting to jump off the swing just a second too soon
At least they swapped out the sand for some rubber surface
I have a plan . . . or at least part of one
I'm going to have a baby, maybe get married
Finish school, sing and dance on stage some more
Sing and dance through life
Make my life something it's never really been
Full of continuous song
One that no one can steal
No matter how mean they are
No matter how much I screw up
No matter whether I live or die
Forever in a state of happy-afraid.

Shannon Murphy

Road's Never Long Enough

Lionel knew I loved to go. He asked me to come to him and help him move. He had spent the summer working in southwestern Utah for some political-cockamamie-I-don't-know-what, getting people to vote or something, almost getting himself killed for trespassing on the property of some jar-pissing lunatic who had painted the words "Keep Out" on a tire and nailed it to a wooden post in his front yard. Not even a "Keep Out" tire would dissuade Lionel from a-knockin'. A gunshot sent him running back before he could reach the door.

"You're lucky he stopped you before you could cross the minefield," I said.

Sometimes I fall for entire neighborhoods, and envy the blades of wind that stir the trees to shimmy. Lionel called as I walked through such a Denver street. "I got into law school at the base of the Blue Ridge Mountains. I'm taking a bed and leaving town. We'll take the 15 through Zion, and I'll sell the mattress in Vegas. With that money, I'll buy a bicycle, and ride to Virginia living off of nothing but dehydrated food and the kindness of trail angels."

The benefits of living on a month-to-month lease in an apartment with no furniture greatly outnumber the drawbacks when one doesn't want to live anywhere in particular. My boss knew I had one foot out the door and never paid me much. I told my landlords to find a new tenant and waited until the end of the month. Then, I gave the remaining contents of my refrigerator to a courteous runaway named Miranda, picked up my things, stuffed them in a sack, and left for the next town.

The old engine of the pickup flapped like a fish in my hands. I drove on to Utah to find Lionel and whatever else I would find there, or along the way. Beached reefs. Martian-hued Godrocks. Jars and bottles of female stone. Yellow mobiles.

Lionelville consisted of a Super 8 and a gas station. The kid had one bag, and he was sitting on it in the motel parking lot, sucking on a straw that led to a strap-on pouch filled with water.

I cranked down the window and declared, "This is no place for a bachelor."

He shrugged.

Lionel is like an inside-out kangaroo. He carries his mother around with him like La Pieta. Instead of smooth legs, he crosses his front teeth. Tall and thin; a tree. Wobbly; a spring. Running. Angry. Always hydrated. We spent one night together, and all he wanted was to show me how easily he could do everything. He never parts with his rattlesnake bravado. I don't know if I like him, but I know that we will remember each other for years. He does great things. He is smart and skilled and not afraid. Yes, he is a man I want to know.

"Marsupial," I say, "Where's the magic bed?"

"In the storage room. I resurrected their hard drive, so they're giving it to me for free."

It took us less than fifteen minutes to load the truck. We dragged the mattress from a closet down a few bent stairs to the gravel parking lot and into the back of the pickup. On the way down the steps, I mowed a lot of white paint splinters off the backbending treads, skeletons reaching up. We threw that rigid sack of springs up over the tailgate, and wriggled it down deep with a lot of ungodly heaving until it rested there in the truck like a tortilla curved against the steel, and then we straightened our legs and panted like marathon runners, lungs flapping.

When it was time to boogie, I said, "You drive, and not like a maniac. I want to lay in the back."

I had a vision of myself like that once: Riding in the open bed of a pickup truck under pregnant calico clouds, sucking down the abalonean wet before it even started to drop. So I climbed into the bed and lay on my back. The truck started to move. The stripped mattress reminded me of what I look like naked, and I pictured us, me and the mattress, as I felt the pre-rain. The sky looked so big I thought it would lick me, and I wanted it to, but it never did. I lived my dream in the back of that truck. My chest got hard in the cold, and the rain didn't fall until after dark, long after I'd crawled into the cab to hear Lionel exclaim, "Your hands are like ice!" But I knew they could not stop the Titanic.

By the time we got to Vegas, he'd already found a guy to whom he peddled the bed. I let the boys unload it.

"So long, old friend," and I gave it a pat. I pointed to the man, whose face I forget: "You'd better put some sheets on that thing."

I told Lionel I'd stay with him for one day as he bought his bike and planned his journey, and talked him into staying at the Circus-Circus hotel.

"Purple carpet!" I promised.

He showed up at the room with brown bags full of groceries and a food dehydrator. His idea of me; a cut chord; Alaskan salmon; the one man he made love to: He preserved these things with the straight mouth of an engineer in our hotel room, not interested in the oppressive whoredom outside, sugar-titted signage blinking not brighter than the dream of his bicycle. He packed the shriveled bricks of provisions, and the next morning sent each to a post office along the Rapunzelean route, and along the way from Las Vegas to the Shenandoah, he'll just add water, piece by piece, kind of like what I was praying for, under the bruised billows in that bed.

At some point, I must have inhaled a chlorine-and-asphalt magnet, because I was back where I swore I'd never be, Los Angeles, by two the next afternoon. I said goodbye to Lionel at nine o'clock that morning, owning faith that he would never change.

Josh Rose

Unopened Buds

Stamens and pollen
Unopened buds
Oil cans and push pins
Bent rulers and blackened bulbs
Squozen tubes of toothpaste
Broken back scorpions and poison pennies
Rusty blades floating in oil
Right angles
Positioned as compass needles for the directionless
The bloody
The razor-thin life we walk
The sad way a boy's life becomes just the dots
And the pencil lines fade between the objects
Handless watches
Fallen stars and a dead shark on the beach
His death like a saint's
The boys cried for innocence
And stayed up all night underneath a bridge
Fearing that if we went to sleep we'd grow old
And so we kissed the girls and sent them home
And the five of us walked the beach
With our razor compasses and Geiger counters
Discovering nails from frostbitten fingers and dead jellyfish sacks
All objects we hold precious eventually become trash
Grandpa's poker chips
Half-eaten album covers and mold containers
The only hope remaining our children
And their unopened buds.

Tim Giblin

BsAs, April 2007

When I lie in bed at night and look at the stars, I wonder—where's my roof
laying nailed to sunk-back joists,
this the cord left that traces chaste pipe
wrapped by a scarf of aluminum,
smoked glass, fossilized faces
striped—bulged—begrudgeoned
fertile threads like tentacled dares.
Chilled fruit stands
and white Chinese aprons.
No means NO
in many languages and the universal hand signal too.
Calvin calvos door knockers
severed appendaged and prolific—
this is what I come back to:
graphic levels with little maps
of rustic love letters
about pine floors, and curbed animals,
all of them racing home screaming
cantos from Pete Seeger fairy tales
about tomorrow and other abandoned singalongs.

Laura Caputo

A Roofless Poem

When I lie in bed at night and look at the stars, I wonder—where's my roof
Where's the top of me and how did I ever lose track
Orion's Belt just on the horizon . . . searching searching for Ursa Major
Cause where there's Ursa Major, off the handle is a bright star named Spica
Spica in Latin means "me"— it doesn't really but it should
'Cause I'm that bright star, the one shining Virgin in the sky
A little extra meat on her bones, a sign of pure health
Hiding the underbelly pains, the family lies
Not lies like shameful secrets, just the untruths we tell ourselves
No means NO
Not opulent, near oblivion, nest old, never offered
I hope that I can live contrary to NO
Life is presenting itself as something different (as of yesterday)
And today although my leg keeps going numb, my heart is full
Even if they say I'm deficient, I'm not
just part of the illusion—
the daytime constellation that's there but you can't see
'cause the sun is too bright to focus past the blue blue blue sky
When I wake in the morning, the sands tangle with the sea
Another roofless night passed, another day of business—unfinished

Mari Weiss

White-hot Flecks

When I lie in bed at night and look at the stars, I wonder—where's my roof?
I can't hear the walls though I feel the floor watching me.
It would devour me if it could,
but then it would have to answer to the bed.

I tried to get up once,
throw back the covers,
climb over the horizon.
My feet never touched the Milky Way
before I was sucked back in.
No means NO
to the soul without YES in its canon.

Still I sing small suns into being
and loose them into the roofless sky
past the silent walls as the floor pants its envy.
The bed is pleased.

I am content.

There is no pain when stars flame out
melting the skin from planets and
burning the bones to ash.
White-hot flecks travel light years to cover the floor, the bed, my eyes.

Leslie Berliant

Where's My Roof

When I lie in bed at night and look at the stars, I wonder—where's my roof.
That's me, I'm the glass-half-empty kind.
The other day, I studied the rusted-out hood of a bronze Cutlass
with its delicate lacy pattern of holes and pock marks.
Clever how it has a second layer of metal underneath to spare the motor.
My roof, my foundation, my walls, they are all rotting
with nothing underneath or outside or above
just dirt and air and stars
which sounds romantic until you mix in rain, worms, spiders, ants and bird shit.
No means NO
unless it means yes.
I can hardly make up my mind these days,
watched so intently by all those sets of prying eyes.
And what makes you so sure that I don't need what she needs?
A man to do man things:
to fix the roof and kill the spiders and take over my life.
Grabbing my ass in front of your escrow guy was so wildly inappropriate.
It was a start.
But it's a shame you are done saving women—
I am lost and could use a little rescuing myself

Vicki Whicker

Magnitude

When I lie in bed at night and look at the stars, I wonder—where's my roof
F5 Tornado, Typhoon 10, Earthquake magnitude 8.4
Something somewhere took it off
And now you can see inside
If you are an angel
If you are my mother
Stopping in to say hello
To say, I am proud of you
For repeating to your son
No means NO
You might also see the dirt
The dust
The tiny nits of unhappiness
What remains of the day
Full catastrophe life
When I lie in bed
I count the stars
1, 2, 3, 4, 5 . . .
And it makes sense
No matter why

Alan Berman

Coordinates

When I lie in bed at night and look at the stars, I wonder—where's my roof?
I've considered domes and decks and beams and bricks
but all I came up with was a wool blanket with an Incan pattern
that, when I soften my focus on it, fuses into a message
of compromise between the dirt and the decision
to leave once for the last time.
North halfway to cynicism; east two moons
to crystal; south a minor third to devotion;
west five fathoms to ambient light. I am asked to explain, but

No means NO
in every language of direction,
in every invocation of the sacred impulse,
in every set of fence posts being driven past
at too high a speed to witness the genuine
moiré that mirrors our velocity
through the physical tomb
for which we have been trained
so well, in such varied patterns,
with incalculable blindness
and the lack of balance it brings.

Tim Giblin

Last Days in L.A., 2006

"When you strike an arc." "What?" she asks "What does 'strike an arc' mean?" I watch her mouth move up and down pushing out words around chewed oatmeal. The fat black Benz clicking minutes by the quarter muncher on Melrose, I try and get away from her face and her mouth and watch a kid skip across the street, the umbrella above the breakfast table makes our little morning here on the street unfortunately civil. I got my index finger on the table, pushing down the front digit into the checkered tablecloth, whispering the way guys who have power tease with their tongue. Breathe, baby Melrose. My finger waits there for hers to join mine, but it doesn't. *When the electrode bears down on the work, the current can't wait—it's beside itself, and it lunges.* I grab her hand that's doddled too long inconsequentially by her saucer, but she pulls it away. "That's called striking an arc. You're putting whatever you're trying to weld in the path of that arc."

Julia Soto Frazer

Virginia

I have a lot to say,
lolling on dogwood blossoms
floating in a birdbath.
My tongue-home—
where the creek baptized me,
metamorphic and cracked on a rocky syllabus
of caramels and purple-veined Indian quartz.
I named them and they
named me; the last one
cherry red like a firecracker
mounted in the sky and held there by
the atmosphere of my mouth.

Day: a smoky trace

Night: the hard moon
chasing me in the backseat of
the Olds, the Nova, and the Santa Maria,
my eyes sleepy under purple shadow.
One never-again moment;
I knew it and held my peace,
my father driving.

Alan Berman

Getting It Covered

I have a lot to say, but I rarely say it
to the microphone in my pillow,
which people wonder about
but I don't actually tell that many.
I figure, if I'm dreaming and talking
and I can get it down, maybe
there will be a way out next time
from the suffocating mobiles
that congest my desert,
cherry red like a firecracker,
glowing blood film covering
those cacti and tortoises, restricting
their growth and motion with
the elasticity of habit, the habit
of bleeding, letting blood.
It's not the only egg up my sleeve,
if you know what I mean, but
it beats hiring someone to stay up
all night waiting for me to say
something or not.

Vicki Whicker

Postage

I have a lot to say
About the path I took to town today
The men I smiled at
The babies I did and didn't have
What lies I believed
And every time I talk
It is to hear myself sing
So that the song sounds the same
But something has changed
Cherry red like a firecracker
Blown to bits then rearranged into something
Less perfect
But easier on the eyes
None of it makes sense
All of it matters
The breeze on my back
Feels like the first kiss
The last heartbreak
The ever-changing price
Of a postage stamp

Mari Weiss

Wal-Mart Love

I have a lot to say—
just nobody to say it to.

There was this guy once,
I guess you could call him my boyfriend.
We used to fuck behind the Wal-Mart
where we worked the 12-to-7 shift.
"C'mon sugar," he'd whisper come break time,
"let's grab a dumpster quickie."
Then he'd sideways smile, all teeth and girl lips,
cherry red like a firecracker.

I liked those lips, wet and soft like a girl.
Not that I ever kissed another girl—
never really wanted to, not until his lips.
Never really wanted anything, not 'til then.

Never really wanted it to stop, not ever.
Not even if he never said my name
or took me to a movie or even bought me a Coke.

One day he just didn't show up for work.
He got fired for stealing—that's what I heard.
I never even got to say goodbye.

Tim Giblin

Uruguay, May 2007

Montivideo felt cleaner and more vivid than before. kneeling on the floor in front of her, the smell and taste of her sweat stuck to my face, her breasts young vessels mounting one on top of the other. The shift of the chips on the gold-balconied roulette table in the lobby. The clarity of 21 years, of her playing music, of her singing, of her leaning back and enjoying Sunday. I looked at myself in the dark stain mahogany mirror of the JC Penny boardroom. A hundred bucks a night including breakfast buffet. Her noxious fume like a blue gun smoke shot from a final round. The chicken bumps on the arc of her leg where it connected to her sex. I looked older but happy, and I remembered being in this city a month before, alone, having tongue vinaigrette at the prix fix lunch on the ground floor. I remembered the way the harbor looked with the rusty tankers and the cargo cranes distended against the smoking stacks of bricks. Maybe not again this capital, this Sunday, this girl, I thought, on my knees, let me breathe it in now and feel my blood in my veins and feel the condensation in my lungs and taste her, really taste her for all she's worth, for all I'm worth, for everything that is now and won't be again.

Laura Caputo

Frame

It's all preserved in a gilded frame
Intentional, mossy, and yellow water-damaged edges
That sly look pasted on top of the big underneath
The big lie, the big tongue, the big deal, the big day
"Come kiss me," but he stands in the door, head cocked to one side
not understanding the implied "please" that went with it
Continued begging, longing for an indigo hello
Hoping for a place in a new frame
And maybe midnight will come and go with not so much as a sailor's sigh
A pale blue door that became something else entirely
a dinner in Venice, succulent succulence
crossword puzzles, trailing brave boredom waves
And beyond the pale, a secret passageway
Dingy flashlights gross girl pardons
Rip it open, plant the seed, not before the summer begins
But in the late spring those earthen 18 days, remember
It cannot be that the memory transformed
is the one about poor Joey falling into his grave
Remind me of death and the dying things,
the old and the new, the string and flat, an impression in the mud

Vicki Whicker

The Little One

It's all preserved in a gilded frame
What should and shouldn't be
We must share this memory
A dead baby
Girl
Torn apart
Into pieces
Hidden in the bushes
By the front door
A pale blue door that became something else entirely
The door to a cave dripping blood
Stalactites and stalagmites with evil little knobs
It's called home
Where live mom and dad and brothers
Who argue and sniff glue and break bones
Black-and-white picture
The family on the front step stiff as Civil War soldiers
The little one
Her arm at mid-salute
It's a cast, not a badge of honor

Mari Weiss

Iron Lung Limbo

It's all preserved in a gilded frame
under glass cracked by constant earthquakes.
I never bolt my furniture to the walls,
it feels like prison enough,
these memories, hazy with layers of greasy years,
muting colors too bright for sore eyes.
Sharp black lines and razor angles still
cut and bleed hot regret over pink faces,
white picket fence, green green lawn and
a pale blue door that became something else entirely.

Reaching for heaven only to wish for hell
when existence becomes an iron lung limbo,
crushing the free-willed limbs
while breathing wicked air into unwanted lungs.
Death would have been easier
but I am not a quitter or a coward.
(no matter what they say)
Someone had to stay behind
to keep the stories true,
to put the fragments under glass and to wait.

Josh Rose

Escobar

It's all preserved in a gilded frame
I walk out of Escobar's house
The dark, Mexican, tequila worn wood
And piñatas mask the undercurrent of tension
Machismo and deadening silken mood.

The evening ends with jar
And the group of us pour
Somewhat like a fan out into the night of promises
To places warmer through
A pale blue door that became something else entirely.

The night is traffic light as I wave them away
But before I can cross the street, pop
The night crawlers open fire on my chest
I feel a sting and before I realize it was only an air gun
The pale blue door for a minute closed.

I've been hit with something and although relatively harmless
Save for what might have become of my eye
It is still in frame.

I'm having a hard time not feeling shot anymore
How long the door? How long the sharp pain?
How long the walk across the street alone?

Shannon Murphy

Middleweight Champions

It's all preserved in a gilded frame.
The gold's slapped on like tar, dripping on
the frosted family like a coming clock.
Airbrushed expressions on greaseless skin,
pale pores cemented, laminated, solid throughout.
No organs. No paper cuts. No hangnails.
Hands neatly folded, burying the triangular edges
of unfiled nails that puncture holes in white paper
maps of photocopied ocean floors and faxed tests.
A pale blue door that became something else entirely:
our planet before it vomited
an atmosphere and Pangaea.
Mom, Dad, brother and sister
surge and crunch, formed and apart,
banded together in a precious cage.
What we need to believe lives mounted above the mantle.
Love is a humming idea that vacuums us in,
strumming serrated limbs like an insect violin,
and then we blast it apart, quarry workers,
scraping colored stone, hunting for quartz and blood.

Leslie Berliant

Escape

It's all preserved in a gilded frame
Eyes squinting, less a smile than a smirk
Looking past the camera
At the one that's been bested
Six-year-old chin on neatly folded hands
Resting on a black leather foot stool
The pointless argument over the pink hand-me-down dress
With the ruffles and the scooped neck
It's a black-and-white photo, after all.
A pale blue door that became something else entirely
In the sepia tone background
That becomes a penetrable sanctuary
Quiet space can be disrupted at any time
By brothers that pick locks
And mothers that take them away entirely
Never to be prevented from entering at will
At all hours
Behind that blue door
Where secret thoughts form in triangular shapes
And I make my plan of escape.

Tim Giblin

Medellin, Day after My 33rd Birthday

barely.....
no, that's being dramatic, I'm here in Medellin, suffering the vast freedom of the tropics, I hear from others it is a dangerous form of anonymity . . . making meetings, praying, and feeling very much connected to the dark forces, the beauty, the death, and the great unknown . . . sound like I'm going to jump off a balcony? Not today, today I'm sober, working on a sculpture, and begging to move into the light, flashes of which I see in the laminates off broken buses, windows that bare destinations, and sometimes a smile from a friendly stranger.
xxoo
tim
——-Original Message——-
>From: "[redacted]"
<[redacted]>
>Sent: Aug 29, 2006 7:23 PM
>To: [redacted]
>Subject:
>You out there?

Josh Rose

I'll See You Tuesday

Black dark skyless
Dirt run blackless
Hard along the rough edge
Hand along the hemline
And stars
A game you break called Habit
Things that are easy that shouldn't be easy
Things that roll forward that you can't stop
Cars Chance Bitterness
Lies you tell
To better live with the lies you live with
And through it all
How to shape a boy into man

I said "Yeah,
I'll see you on Tuesday."
He said, "What day is today?"
I said Sunday.
He counted to himself:
"Monday, Tuesday, that's the day after tomorrow."
I said, "That's right."
He kept smiling as he disappeared into the house
The house with the sidewalk I used to park in front of
And now just leave the motor running

As I leave she asks if I could pick up Taco Bell
She says for the first time
Sex is like it is in her fantasies
I pick up the food and *Bullit*
And I spend the night explaining all the reasons she should
Fall for Steve McQueen
And not for me
She says she's never had sex with a guy
Who could last an hour
And I want to believe I'm a man

Who would lean forward
Over the handle bars of a motorcycle
Who could say *That's bullshit*
In a way that ends conversations
Not starts them
But she's 26
And grew up idolizing Leonardo DiCaprio
So what does she know?

Last night I read funny poems to Noah
From *Where the Sidewalk Ends*
And afterward I said I had bought this other book
It was way below his reading level
One of those thick cardboard ones with only about 12 pages
And I was embarrassed to say that I got it for him
So I said it was for his little sister
It was called *I Love You All the Time*
And I read it anyway
And he fell asleep with his hand on my arm

I'm obsessed with a photograph of Peter Beard
The one of him lying on a beach
Writing in his journal
While the lower half of his body appears to be being eaten
By a giant crocodile
However I'm pretty sure that piece will set me back about
Twenty thousand dollars
And I already spent that this year
Learning how to be a man again

My mother and I went to go see the Harrison Ford remake
Of *The Fugitive* when it came out
And afterward she said
Women want a man like Tommy Lee Jones
What she really meant was that she wanted a man like Tommy Lee Jones
But she didn't know how to raise a boy
So she used the resources available to her
Movies and books
So that
To this day
Whenever she recommends one to me
I still feel like I'm getting another lost jigsaw

Of a thousand-piece puzzle
She keeps locked away behind that wooden door

As the car idles
Out where the sidewalk ends
Noah and I recap all the best parts of our weekend
The walk in Venice
The drive up the coast
Westwood with
The racing games
And the stories
He said he liked the funny poems
I said I liked that other book we read too
The one called *I Love You All the Time*
He said, "That's my sister's book."
I looked up into the rearview mirror
He was smiling to himself as he looked out the window
I said "Yeah.
I'll see you Tuesday."

Laura Caputo

Lady Lee: Part 1

I am brilliant.
Today I took an online test
and I ranked in the top half of
women my age who are still blessed
with a healthy sexual drive.
I tell you it is quite an amazing experience
to be so well lubricated
when all of my friends are either dried up or dead.
The men are quite interesting themselves.
Since I started dating again,
I have found that there are more men looking
for a woman to take care of them
and hold their hand
than the kind I am looking for.
And it is quite clear to me
that just as my female companions
have lost their sexual urges,
so too, have these male counterparts.
It's much easier
to meet the right kind of man
down at the Lyons Club socials
or the hotel lobby pubs than online.
I suppose it's not politically correct
for a woman to want it as much as a teenage boy,
but what can I say?
Neither here nor there, I suppose.
This older gentleman, Gary, and I
spent last evening at the Rhumba club
dancing until 11 P.M.
He dropped me off at my apartment
but he would not come in for a nightcap.
I suppose he was tired
and had plans early the next morning,
so I simply went next door
and played Chinese Checkers with Henry,
among other things.

As much as I enjoy Henry,
he's just not very good in bed.
I'm headed over to the community center tonight
for some Bingo,
usually a bunch of old biddies
but I'm ready to make some real money.
I can hardly still believe last year my luck.
I won $5000 and a limo for one week.
It was quite wonderful
going to the grocery store with my limo.
And the limo driver, Berniece, was such a sweet doll.
She was a wonderful girl
trying to pay for her little daughter's private schooling.
We got along famously.
She and I went to the Lotus car dealership
and test drove cars for a few hours.
I hadn't met any gals before Berniece
who enjoyed cars as much as I have over my 82 years.
Here's a poem I wrote yesterday:

When your male friend asks you in for a drink or two
Tell him why, yes, but that it's not something you normally do
If he asks if he can give you a kiss
Turn your cheek and say why, yes, but don't miss
When he plants a wet one on your cheek
Tell him it's your turn—ask him to close his eyes and not peek
If he says yes, now is your chance
Lean in close and tear off his pants
If he says no, simply stand up and walk away
He was never meant to be, he's probably not a good lay . . . anyway.

Leslie Berliant

Late Night on *HSN*

I just want to know if you're in or out
If you're man or machine
If your mustache is real
or spray-on hair from an aerosol can
electric food dehydrator dial-o-matic bagel cutter
pocket fisherman inside the shell egg scrambler godammit
What have I done?
The only thing I ever invented, oh, let's not go there.
It's all detritus now, anyway. Detritus I tell you. Detritus
With a capital 'D'
For deliverance from the garbage heap
The things (people) we desire
And then cast away
The people (things) we order up
In a late-night insomniac frenzy
They don't shine so bright in the daytime
Never did, never have
But oh, that bottle of gin sure helped him glow
Those lines of coke sure made his skin feel soft against mine
His cock hard, his greed full and sharp, my fingers poised to dial.

Tim Giblin

Patagonia

In the stillness of my deep dark cavernous
tuxedo-shaped heart
she translated the words of Neruda
with the disclaimer that he was soft
"Es tan corto el amor, y tan largo el olvido"
in her odd timing and abrupt silences.
I had the wool binding stitched battleship grey
by the mother of lost names whose patron saint
opens windows and bus station
sunsets. We made no plans for later.
Yippee! Yippee! I say, while they stare
at me funny?
and charge this vile voice slander,
more here with glaciers prehistoric blue
and steaks weighted blood,
dangled in chalky waters for a bite.
She was telling me about her divorce
because I demanded the contractor's
intimate details. She claimed ten years'
worth and I wanted to fillet his words
from her white meat and snatch up the bones
before the gulls' eyes even woke.

Julia Soto Frazer

Betty Rubble

In the stillness of my deep dark cavernous tuxedo-shaped heart
I slow dance in light baby blue. Polyester
ringlets, shiny and tight,
crashing hopelessly, relentlessly like a Nancy Drew character into a
pale, shaded boyfriend that I will leave for a new pit-mate.
I never understood the Betty Rubble of it all,
the rules of the Mystery of the Broken Engagement,
the fondness of two people for the
hopeless, relentless clichés that last a lifetime.

Yippee! Yippee! I say, while they stare at me funny.
I'm in a man's suit with false eyelashes
strapped on and speed listening to
Sun Ra on Avenue A at 3:00 A.M. in a Manhattan ballroom.
It was the life I wanted and
I got it, half-priced at Blimpies with
bedbugs from Bowery futons and
pickles in barrels
and one musician after another and one after
that and me after that, tucked into a chamber,
prolapsed and pounded into glittering, laughing bits.

Vicki Whicker

Chuck Close Repeat

In the stillness of my deep dark cavernous tuxedo-shaped heart
Is a room with pictures of everyone I have lost
Mother, mother, grandmother, grandmother, mini-portraits in grid squares
Chuck Close repeat until the walls are like a fly's multicolored eyes
And if I squint, get my vision to blur, I can see me
Uno, one, only, me, just me
Thank God I didn't have a daughter to sink
Into the quagmire, into the mess, baby Mastadon into the tar pits
Not so bad looking covered with black goo
Yippee! Yippee! I say, while they stare at me funny
In the stillness of my deep dark cavernous tuxedo-shaped heart
I sit in a room filled with pictures of every boy man that I ever slept with
First love, first love, last love, last love, those two pictures Chuck Close repeat
Until the walls are like a fly's multipictured eyes
And if I squint, get my vision to blur, I can see me
Uno, one, only, me, just me
Thank God I didn't have a daughter to sink
Into the quagmire, into the mess, baby Mastadon into the tar pits
Not so bad looking covered with black goo
Yippee! I say, to nothing, to no one, to me

Alan Berman

Steps

In the stillness of my deep dark cavernous tuxedo-shaped heart
is an example of how I described things when I was a kid,
all drama and bluster. Now I'm dull: I think,
The usual lack of risk that precedes doing the dishes.
The result is the same, after all: solitude is forgotten only
by those who have something else.
I am creating mechanisms to forget mine.
I remember how I beat it once, for just a moment.
I reenact it now, in front of the photos on my dresser:
"Yippee! Yippee!" I say, while they stare at me funny;
at least I imagine their stares. They're all dead now,
dead to whatever laughs I can bring them,
sticking my fingers into my nostrils,
crossing my eyes, pinching my lips between my teeth
and filling my cheeks with air.
None of this is funny to me anymore:
the only reason I ever laughed at it
was that others would. I took my cues
from the ones whom I needed
to make me feel alive.

Mari Weiss

a well-done day

diddle dee crackpot
hey there, you!
keep dancing that jiggity gee
i could climb a tree
or a rope with a knot
that would swing out over the lake
splishity splash i'd be taking a bath
with a giggle and a hop and a screech
when my tippity toes
hit the friggity cold
swoosh
stroke
breath
f l o a t
mmm sunny sun sun
warms my tummy tum tum
while i float
like a boat
cross the big blue sea
no, not a sea
silly willy
but blue cool lake
where i bake
on the sandy sand
between dips in the pool

floppity flop flip-flops
smack and slap
across hot black tar de har har
hot hot
ow ow ow
that's whattcha get
dashing in bare feet
such a hurry to get the
purple
cherry

orange
SURPRISE!
ice cream popsicle treaty sweet
sweet reward for
a job well done
a day well spent
a well-done day

well well well
what have we here and
there and everywhere you look
it's green and grain
and sun and rain
and rainbows in my
hair down to there
in pigtails
braids
up down
and all around
did i show you my two-step?
it's getting good good goody
good as gold
right as rain
could you sing that song again?
i love to dance
i surely do do dee doo
wait!
would you?
sing that song again?
i love that tune
like the mooney moon moon
so yellow hello and full of
love makes the world go round
you are my world
go round
please?
for me?

Alan Berman

Too Late

I wish I had never met him,
is all I remember from the recording
done that evening by someone I, frankly,
wish I had never met, because if I hadn't met her,
she would have never put me in contact with
the guy who said that he wished he'd never met me,
and there'd be no such stealthy negative sentiments
passing through this infospace that was her idea.
I believed things would be different with her, but
she was another story—
a question I had dismissed upon meeting her—
but then she struck. Never
could I say no to such a request.
I even remember telling myself
when I was a kid watching reruns of *Petticoat Junction*:
I will never say no to a beautiful woman.
Such thinking saved me from questioning myself,
like eating only foods on a certain diet:
shopping goes more quickly; confidence feeds itself.
I owe her a call.

Laura Caputo

Made Up

And when the people had come and gone,
had come and gone
from a day
an evening
a century of suffering and oppression,
when that day was over and they left a trail . . .
that is when I began to pick up my bones and skin.

It is when I opened up my naked eyes with the lids gone,
exploded away. I saw and felt everything
from that day on that I ever needed to know
to survive in this world
to live my most authentic tragic days
without sorrow or woe.
I am living proof that the sun is still shining
even if its light is a little dimmer now.
I made it all up
from clay and twigs,
from ink and cowhide,
from grey cabinet doors to bamboo hallways . . .
I made it . . . crafted it.

There were stories and seashells
that whispered the truth and the lies
of what happened
when that century
that day
that evening
erupted
and volcanic lava laughter sprayed them down . . .
way before the earth ever heated over . . .
it turned its insides out
and I remain here all alone
with trash and pillow feathers to sleep on
under the muffled up and down rumbling of the land below,
I made it . . . inside . . .

Julia Soto Frazer

Journal Entry—February 6, 1972

I wonder if I will ever get to be an FBI agent
and if I don't
I can always be a writer.

Alan Berman

Follow-Through

"An ominous dark delivery, Mr. Rose. Like a flapjack."
My cat jumped from the fireplace mantle
just as I closed the door behind him.
"Our arrangement is satisfactory to you?"
I knew the answer before I spoke.
I learned that from Father.
We sat at the mahogany table.
"It is light," I said. "Should I be concerned?"
He looked away, then down at his left hand. His turn.
"Hey, when are we gonna get 1 and 10 from you, Slick?"
he said. I knew his routine. This was fair.
But I had a surprise for him.
"I work for myself now," I said.
I inhaled, but not as quietly as I'd planned.
He didn't break his avoidance of eye contact.
"Give my best to Charlotte," he said.

After he left I went back to the table,
hoping the phone would ring.
It wasn't what I expected.
It was too late to call it a mistake.

Mari Weiss

Hungry Gods

An ominous dark delivery, Mr. Rose, like a flapjack
browned and a little greasy without
the sticky politeness of "Howdy ma'm."
Standing at inattention waiting for god only knows what.
Except deities don't do much talking these days
choosing, instead, to email their sacrificial requests.
Sorry NOT DELIVERABLE to those in need LOL be sure to write
Not-so-winged messengers appear in dark alleys, on lousy sitcoms,
at the front door, knocking loudly and demanding,
"Hey, when are we gonna get 1 and 10 from you, slick?!
While you're at it, throw in some bacon—
those deities love their bacon!"
Lips smacking at the thought,
thoughts smacking at the third eye,
craving escape to fly up to Heaven Valhalla home.
But they are too heavy with fatty tears and want
so they land flatly at steel-toed feet. Mr. Rose
puts them out of their misery with a snort and a two-step,
tired of the game. The gods look up from their keyboards,
watching him relent, knowing they will go hungry again.

Vicki Whicker

dastardly day

an ominous dark delivery mr rose, like a flapjack
smothered in chokeberry syrup
the kind we eat on the porch out back
jawing the 152-pound catfish
that killed that haynes kid, other side of the track
pulled him under, remember
on the longest day of the year, heck
june 21, always a dastardly day
or why old lady randall killed her man when he said, *you old wreck*
hey, when are we gonna get 1 and 10 from you slick?
she'd done run out of grins
took his bull chain and wrapped it around his thick skull and with a kick
threw him in the slew
let him drain long in the pond
brings me back to damn catfish
always itching to eat yuck
rooting around for fingers and toes
in the slimily murk
how they'll find you, rose—
hell knows it'll be a lot of work

Julia Soto Frazer

Irish Breakfast

An ominous, dark delivery, Mr. Rose, like a flapjack,
like a little, flip-flapping paddy whack bone.
Oh, gluten thud of meta-Sundays and
me in the kitchen with James Joyce twistin' hay;
I've got tiny globs of syrup fish-eyed
on my cherry flannel thighs when the lads
blast the kitchen to smithereens and
send me shooting through the chimney
Up, swing set! Up, gallows! Up . . .

Hey, when are we going to get 1 and 10 from you, Slick?

Go ahead—I'll catch it up here—
the view's grand for a touch of
beginning and middle—
the end, I know already.
I'm green
I'm tamped
I'm peat in an oven
for potato boyos to outlast
the demesnes of sandwich earls
as worn as my Da's pajamas.

Laura Caputo

Oh, the Games We People Play

I have a dungeon. It is filled with torture devices.
First, I capture the enemy—the offender—and chain it to the walls.
Then stripping piece by piece—dignity, integrity, respect, happiness,
the calm, peace for mankind,
shirt and trousers, underwear, and hat—
gone, stripped, stripped away, and hidden or sometimes burned.
Next, I put on the mask, the masks, the pathetic faces of someone who
    doesn't even exist
Sometimes I paint them on, sometimes I bolt them on.
Tied, stripped, and invisible that's how I make it happen.
And this is just how it begins. There's more of it to come.
Surprises in store for the prisoner. Humiliation and neglect.
How to achieve a rich life of coffee grinds, apple cores, and meat
dangling off the bone. It's my favorite book that I have yet to write.
I know what the second chapter will be about already
and the fifth will start with "the crying out from under a gag
of wet tissues soaked in brown and yellow turtle dung . . ."
The clock ticks but you can't see it. Time's passing but the hand's still at 4,
the sun never comes up, the cock does not crow, the cock shrieks.
Remember when we used to walk to school? Remember when we had rocks
thrown at our heads? Remember when we—I had nothing to keep up with
the Joneses, the Jerry Joneses, the Jerry Joneses who molested little boys,
the little boys in the cubscouts? And remember, how we—
I can peel the skin from your toes, the stuff that's left, after I pull off the nails?

It's not me, silly . . . don't you remember?
I hear the muffled voice of a child, too—that bitch. And finally, the
    whipping, the whip,
the whip, the whipping—only to be executed after the shock, the tweezing
    of body hair
to prepare, and the yoga that stretches the captured in half. It's not all of what
    happens down there, but you get the point. I have a dungeon.
I have a dungeon. It is filled with torture devices.

Tim Giblin

Baja, May 2006

He pointed south to La Paz, south towards peace where things that are broken bang the guardrail of the Sea of Cortez's skinny ramp, the baby brother of the darker cousin. "It'll take a week," Rojellio said, talking about a bunch more problems other than the ground cog of 4th gear. There's a Clausing gang press, and a nice old ideal arc that launches 300 amps from a libertine green wand ignited only by impatient proximity. "It's a remote start," I say, dragging my burnt fat digit on the transformer's heavy dial. I am a spy with different voices for different stages: a doctor's son at the dining room table, under Chagalls and Roualts, a loose-lipped sandaled wifebeater on Bedford, an Avedon-creased sun drifter by the 28th Parallel. "Sorry for the muted lies I can't help but tell," I say, then strike.

Leslie Berliant

Salt and Skin

I woke up in the morning, bruised and, for the first time, no parents
ringing in my head, asking to be disobeyed.
I fought for years to get them out of there, I have to admit
they were unrepentant squatters.
4 A.M. with a hard-on pushed up against me,
it wasn't quite anybody's morning but mine.
What are you supposed to do with that
if you are an insatiable insomniac?
Turns out there's only one answer
Turns out you can be strong and still not be courageous
Turns out you can't stay emotionally disconnected forever.
I had avoided all the *fuck me's* and *harder, harder's*
for a whole month
but one slipped out in my restlessness and daze.
He tried to deliver the pound, pound, pound of my past
but his discomfort and my outdated needs made me sad.
Slowing down, he put a hand under my shoulder blades
pulling me closer
kissing my eyes closed
until all I could taste was salt and skin.

Julia Soto Frazer

1972

I woke up in the morning, bruised and, for the first time, no parents,
radio speaker imprint on my cheek.
It was the Kinks, I think—
they made me do it
they made me forget everything:
family, friends, the fact that I was only eleven.
Music does that to a person;
it makes you go Manson on yourself
in a printed mini and the layered look.
Turns out you can be strong and still not be courageous.
You can go to school
slam your locker
pass your tests
and shirk the walls with pig's blood,
wearing raving mad hatter thrift shop
silks and sparkle haircuts,
stepping into used suede boots that
smell like an old woman who used to be you.

You know it's true because you are her now
and nothing but the hollowing cheek ever changes.

Shannon Murphy

Miracle Desert

I woke up in the morning, bruised and, for the first time, no parents.
There's an eerie quiet that no slam shakes. Not any clickclickclick can make the sounds
I need to hear, except for my heels in the ground. And away this time, not around.

If a family's like a solar system, my folks were all the generations of forget-me-not astronomers who re-interpreted the cosmic waltz to spite each other,
and then compared it all to a loaf of bread. I learned quick to never laugh at their talking over each other. Traffic. Gridlock. Six generations of Californians,
we've got asphalt in our blood. Lava hardens around a redwood truck.
Recessive genes pave blue roads. Rivers be dammed.

Turns out you can be strong and still not be courageous
(or something along those bloodlines.)
Ah hell, who am I kidding, I need my family to live!
And besides, I've called myself worse things than a coward.

I arrowhead my skeleton, and lay beside the girl in the drawer. In this museum,
we spoon like the remains of Pompeii. Across the street, a painting bleeds.
See him.

He gives birth to eclipsed sons, beautifully confused, and tries to give back
the breath he took. And down the street, the greatest sandwich of all time.

In the end, I guess all I'll leave behind is this evidence.
Bruises resembling the continents out of order: some skin, a miscalculated map of home.

Mari Weiss

Losing Bet

I woke up in the morning, bruised and, for the first time, no parents.

Wait, did I just say "parents"?
Wow—talk about your Freudian slip.

I felt like I was on the losing end of a bet.
Guess all they wanted was a pound of flesh.
That and my pants, which were nowhere to be seen.

Christ, do I live here?
If I do, I have piss poor taste.

My mouth taste like lies, my knuckles raw—oh yeah,
turns out you can be strong and still not be courageous.
All that running must have caught up with me.
Sure as shit someone was faster
and bigger and smarter and . . .
pissed.

Wouldn't be the first time.
If I had a talent for anything, it was that.
The only gift my parents gave me,
a meager inheritance from a lousy bloodline
that will end with me—thank god!

I went back to sleep, relieved and, for the first time, no dreams.

Vicki Whicker

Cottonmouth Youth

I woke up in the morning bruised, and for the first time, no parents
I woke up for the second time with no kid, just an empire of sand
Left turn signal click tick stuck
Dizzy head to dangling toe
Cactus stop sign
A different vanishing point for each eye
Cottonmouth youth
Soaked in bloody oil
The sighs of the dying
Turns out you can be strong and still not be courageous
Turns out I need all of my bones
Because the shin bone is connected to the knee bone
Because the knee bone is connected to the past
So that even if I see two simmering silk horizons
I can't get there
Dumb shit
Why go so fast with so little road
Dime store Icarus
Tried for the stars, retard
Tried too hard

Tim Giblin

Rio, January 2007

I take motobike cabs up and down the hill, but at night the switchbacks are invisible and the only way I know we are going up, is 'cause I hear the two-stroke strain against my thighs and I watch over my shoulder where the ocean makes polkadot victims out of faint cargo ships bobbing in the harbor. I like it here, it's like Bed-Stuy on a Saturday night. I've got a studio with a view of Sugarloaf. I met a girl in NYC when I was home, and when I kissed her I swear it all went white. My mind the night sky, her lips like a Hiroshima blast full of burning babies and scarred flesh. I thought of sweet diesel, and the East River drive. She made me want to go fast, and get shipwrecked in her cab ride home. I forgot everything about Brazil, and Sundays by myself and whatever else got left behind. I'm using Rio like a bandaid now, and for the moment it's still working.

Julia Soto Frazer

The Genealogy of Food

I said, Take out the brain,
cracker barrel boy,
and slice it thin
with a heavy hammer of fun.
Slop heavy gravy bowl,
crunchy goodness of
calibrated scone dip,
eagle-eyed jellybeans
and tangled thumbprint urges

it was the best food I've ever eaten
and still I complained

Pomegranate seed Persephone with
thigh crisp spread,
lamb shanks trembling hard wheat,
spun sugar merry-go-round,
crazy-eight eggs stiff peaked,
prudent and dry,
like tiny Basque nuns
gliding spitfire through
my matrilineal veins.

Leslie Berliant

Lost Weekend at the Ritz

The brass door handles to the patio are cocked at different angles,
one straight across, one up and to the left at 45 degrees.
It appears to me that one may be broken, but they both work
and the doors open to a wood deck secluded by trees and
green plants.

We leave the curtains open to the late afternoon
while listening to Brahms,
the sun streaming in through the glass doors.
I am—*we* are; I must get used to this new pronoun
We are in a painting, full color, unlike the muted tones and hunting party
above us.

The moon is up by the time we are hungry for anything more.
It is insatiable, this need, my need
wide awake after a slumber that seemed too long at the time
but turns out to have been just long enough.

I say "Tell me again"
and am shocked every time
at the lack of conditions
as the words move from my ears
to my brain
to the tips of my fingers.

I already dread Sunday night
leaving the hotel
where they address me as "Mrs."
where I am perfect for a day.

In a life of self-sufficiency
it is rare as summer frost
this being cared for
with dinners and whispered words and high-thread count white cotton sheets.

I feel lost as we walk through gardens and museums
and pick out art for the walls

but he seems to know where we are going
and is willing to show the way.

It's something I could get used to:
this lost, this man,
this easy acceptance,
this quiet clarity,
this love.

Mari Weiss

hazel-colored sorrow

crumpled sheets futon
laundry—clean and not so—surround
champagne poetry afternoons lost
then and now
never again
sweet Sunday morning ritual
still practiced religiously
strong coffee the *Times*
(New York nothing else)
lazy bed musky heaven
still my favorite morning
Sunday

John Hiatt, Marshall Crenshaw
Oscar Peterson, Mel & Ella & Elvis
(new and old)
Frank
"the ears of my ears awaken"
did you give me e. e. too?
more music and books than furnishings
and a cat named Jones
(Smith the dog lived upstairs)

cognac candled bath ready
in the late hours after
I lived the dream
that you watched
with tortured artiste eyes
don't you know how I suffer?
I do, darlin', I do
and I'd take it away if I
had a heart big enough
I thought it was
but neither of us had enough
strength for the loss

it joined us from the first
over drinks—we forgot to eat
lost in the finding
you gave me a song
and I dissolved into
hazel-colored sorrow
not knowing just how
it would have its way

bear of a presence father
leaves a gaping hole
the wayward son cannot begin to fill
"He's gone"—4 A.M. call
there on the futon
arms enfold amid laundry and loss
there are tears—only then
not in the days ahead
something else slips in
unnamed to this day

cathedral arched incense
ritual of another kind
a bishop and cardinals
and the throngs
he was beloved
I am a stranger to all
but the one who needs me
drifting in the shadows
staying busy—useful

"Come down" he whispers
tiptoe past family to the sofa bed
where he fills the indent left behind
I am shy. "We can't"
"We have to"—those eyes
I haven't the strength
the room so quiet we swallow our tears
le petit mort
it was the end of us
in the days to come
a slipping away
a phone call—no more
okay
no tears—not ever
I still have the song

Josh Rose

Plastic cup spit up blood

This was roughly the same path backwards
Where the devil rain burns your eyes
Over stickly burrs in a mucus jungle
For the love of hurky boars and punch drunk apes
We slept inside each other
Though we never knew each other
You were my stand-in mother
And I the father you never knew
And the shower we took never inside us cleaned
Later, by myself
From a hotel's plastic cup
I spit up blood
And carved the wood beneath my bed
In a little Javanese town
Knowing I'd never see this place again
Not knowing if that's good or bad
And that is the limitation of man
That for all the circuitry and flying machines
All the feeling emotion and all the biblical explanations
There are three things our minds will never know.

Alan Berman

Soul-Sitting

Sometimes you have to feed the monster;
other times you have to pretend it isn't there.
I haven't always known the rules—
I'm a late starter. I have
calluses that pulse on my vertebrae
and that's how I know when it's time
to learn a new one on the list.

The first time I felt that suggestion,
I knew it was time to name the monster.
Sometimes it's just so predictable;
at least, that's what the others think.
Anything that takes time to reveal the details
they say is *boring*. The only boring thing
is what they probably do every single hour.
Give me true boredom any day,
the lowest down-time you've got.
Then I'll forge my own sustenance
out of the decay around me,
the way I want it,
the way that reveals my name.

Vicki Whicker

Typhoon Party

Sometimes you have to feed the monster
How I loved you back when, with your GQ model pose
And your Hugo Boss summer weight suits
With your Davidoff Blue Water scent
Oh, you kissed my Bono earrings right off my ears
There you were on my first business trip to Hong Kong
Drunken kisses in a cheap Kowloon Hotel
White-collared criminal trying to shuck the life right out of me
Harbour View, yes, but a Holiday Inn nevertheless
Sometimes it's just so predictable
Third trip, you left me with my red print on your handsome Aussie jaw
Slapped for drunk dancing with a Brit, Club 1997, typhoon party, D'Aguilar
Street, 1989
Silly American, I followed you into the Typhoon 10
But you disappeared into a wall of warm rain and there I was
Between lightning flashes and rolling thunder
Unable to find the front door of the bar again
Somewhere between the dead cat with the wonky eye
And the dented white van filled with drunken Chinese sailor men
Before Victoria Harbour and her petticoated surrender
I learned—sometimes you feed the monster, most times you eat him

Laura Caputo

Happy Days

These are happy days
The days of wine and chocolate feathers
I have one foot on the ledge and one foot out the door
I sing a song of sixpence
Tread water for a little over five lifetimes
And then a man comes and opens up the gates
The floods separate the good from the bad
My heart from my bone-crushing fists
And there is no question about who's going up in the rapture
The fat lady's singing a duet
One voice from her right thigh, the other coming out her ass
We swing from vines and up and down the merry-go-round
I can't take all this joy
Tonight I'll sit on the sidelines and scream for the other team
Tonight I'll bask in the glory of the last setting sun
Tonight I'll think of the things that I left for the tomorrow that never comes
Tonight I'll bake cookies and eat them for the neighbors I never met
Tonight I'll read the poems I never understood and understand them
Tonight I'll masturbate to the faces of the men I wouldn't let myself love
Tonight I'll decide bridge or rope and end these happy days for good.

Leslie Berliant

Stale Sheets

On the train, New York to Boston, he barked...
like a top-hatted ringmaster
and I fell for his *All aboard—*
train's leaving the station
and you best be on it, no looking back
so damn seductive with that accent of his.

I road those rails backwards, *Times* in hand,
from the urbane to the provincial
Battery Park 36th floor with a door man to a College Ave. walk-up
in Somerville

This is where I slept last night, the smell of stale cigarettes on my hair . . .
Dakaar Noir drowning the stained sheets, giving me a headache
of magnificent proportions
or was that the combination of white powder and tannic red wine?

In Battery Park, everything smells like money
and chestnut vendors and sewage-riddled river water.
In Somerville, it all smells like stale sweat and sex,
intoxicating enough to make a girl forget why she left
this city, this bed, this man once, twice, third times the charm.

I take the train back to New York where
the streets are dirty but the sheets are clean.

Julia Soto Frazer

Nags Head

Salt water is not good for flowers or eyes
or anyone over forty-five.

Conch shells, my moody joy
forever in black and white photos,
my father balding in the background,
forever Nags Head, forever ocean,
forever my body perfect and sandy,
Venus-frothed in a storm bikini,
sixteen and counting.

But my acceptance speech is penned, much feigned gratitude extended
much false hope projected
into a jawless future, jawless like a lamprey
before screws were invented
and hinges secured words
and orthodontists cashed in.
I was no landlubber and
my webless, unfortunate toes
beat furiously against drumstick boyfriends
and halter-top girls popped into drive-in trunks.

Nags Head forever, my sweet, salt water sixteen.

Alan Berman

State of Affairs

Salt water is not good for flowers. Or eyes.
Five'll get you ten that it's not a good aphrodisiac either:
just try it on a pair of fucking snails.

Look, I've been through all but the part
you think I've been through. I'm here only
because a friend can't be; no one wants
someone who has real reason to be as down
as most of us let ourselves become, in a luxury of misery.
Meet him, and you'll feel good about your whole life, start to finish.

But my acceptance speech is penned, much feigned gratitude extended:
I am for you, certain and capable.
I'm listening now to the music I want you to like
after we've been together many more hours,
after I've learned all your rules and satisfied
all the conditions all your formers forced you to cultivate
like herbs on your precautionary sill.
I think I'll stop there—but look what's growing now, sweetheart:
a crooked, pale stem that will resist being inside your bay view.
It will grow without your help and attention
and will remind you how you got here in the first place.

Leslie Berliant

Acts of Love

Salt water is not good for flowers. Or eyes.
Or shiny pennies. Or decaying bodies.

Or delaying the inevitable, snuffed out too soon.
But they say it can cleanse the guilty of their sin.
I wonder if when the burden carried is so great
the cleansing will be
a walk into the ocean
with stones in pockets.

They like to say that a person dies peacefully, it's a lie.
But my acceptance speech is penned, much feigned gratitude extended.
So glad I could be there for you, thanks for letting me into your pain.
Thanks for sharing the images that you can't erase
that I can't erase
that no amount of salt water can erase.
I want to pour the sharp solution into my eyes anyway
but blinding won't mute the visions of

one side of her body already dead, a few more hours of pain left
begging three times for the unavoidable ending of 16 years.
Now every time I close my eyes, I see that last futile struggle
and a mother's terrible act of love.

Mari Weiss

Black Thumb

Salt water is not good for flowers. Or eyes.
Salt tears, though, clear away the crust
of a million filthy megapixels that scream past my cornea
and smear my fervent brain with the muck of humanity.
It is persuasive compost, bringing even puny notions
into violent bloom. Not my doing.
My black thumb is only good for hitching into the loops
of my clever jeans. I'm no whoreticulturalist
though I've made a few things grow in my time.

But my acceptance speech is penned, much feigned gratitude extended,
and basking in the glory would seem only fair.
Ha! Fair-haired blue-eyed Aryan doppelganger bitch.
No salt-water tears shed there.
So what if I didn't Johnny Appleseed on acid see-ed?
My blood sweat filled those furrows, thicker than H_2O
and just as potent a ferment.
Black is as good as green to myopic sheep.

Why bother? Jeans hitched, thumb out, no one to save but myself.
I have to take credit where credit is due.
Overdue. Long.

Vicki Whicker

Perfect Bones

Salt water is not good for flowers or eyes
Peanut butter is not best in chocolate cups
A Snickers bar and a cold Coke anchor
Technicolor *Playboys* stolen from adults
Sage green summer day and a strong need to be left alone
Untouched by adults or nerdy neighbors
Rock 'n' roll cutoff jeans
Winston hard-pack
Long legs need no audience
But my acceptance speech is penned, much feigned gratitude extended
Many pretend bouquets stripped of thorns
Beyond rules behind the barn
Gravity has no purchase with
Perfect bones
DNA of a summer cloud
Teenage girl with
Plenty of later time
For the crash of accumulation
Soon enough the polluted ocean
Of middle-aged eyes

Josh Rose

Salt Water

Salt water is not good for flowers—Or eyes
But I saw last night where it's good for pock marks
And scars left over from acne
Only they don't say Salt Water
They say Saline Solution.

Just like yesterday
She didn't say you were right
She just asked to borrow money
And cried crocodile saline solution
But my acceptance speech is penned
Much feigned gratitude extended
To my mother who taught me to laugh
Where laugh is another word for angry lion blood kill
To my father who taught me to be confident
But only through the self-injected sea water
To fill in the cavities of emptiness
That were chipped out every night salty-eyed
In the top bunk
With nobody
Not even a bed
Below.

Tim Giblin

Colombia, August 2006

My heart skipped a beat, one pulse left, a free man
I saw her there, death, my maiden, my woman
I found her
I've been thinking about white porcelain coral
chained to a black wax blanket with gold cuffs.
A coral virgin with broken teeth
all of it the dissolving anode,
me on the bottom of a rolling pin hull,
flattening down a path to the end
god there, filling my heart with things of beauty
and the black broken glass in tar
stuck to the sides of my broken intestine,
all of it together, frozen in a lily-white apothecary,
a buoy marking this last and only step,
this one out from lostness towards her,
my foot on the floor stepping
a Columbian bar dark and full of teeth,
mine sharper than everyone's, god-given, god-taken away,
all of it my Atlantic nest, my broken anode, my arc catcher,
my sunken treasure. My destiny.

Laura Caputo

The Nature of Concrete

Tortured animus belies the worthy controvert
Writhen for the sake of her enemies
She left home 10 years ago maybe more
No longer does she seek a remedy
Instead nothing but ripostes
Like the fast snatch of a frog papillae palette
Hiking up her skirt to show her scars her rocks
Falling over herself to be valid in a universe of iniquity
Entombed hope impaled somewhere in the core
Maybe closer not so deep but in the magma
Sugarcoated enmity drafts in the tracks of truth
The question remains, who is her primordial foe
And further still, how much venom and from where
Every forward tread, a stabbing torment shakes her soul
Tortured, yes, a common condition
Worthy, of course, the privilege of prevailing seasons
Constant years of the same broad scowl, monster eyes, craggy skin
Laundering shirts and sheets without fail
This despoliation of existence extinguishing her marbles
And I am not so foolish to believe she will ever change

Leslie Berliant

When the Circus Comes to Town

Tortured animus belies the worthy controvert
blind, truth gets caught in a deluge of hail
she runs for cover, but too late
pounded into the ground, into nothing
she whispers *stop*
at the whistle stop
where chanters and miscreants
congregate beneath the eaves
singing *holy, holy, holy.*

Sugarcoated enmity drafts in the tracks of truth
deaf, dumb and blind to the specter
rather taken by the spectacle
of the bread and circus
where truth had a ring side seat,
were truth still alive to take it,
having paid quite dearly for her ticket.

A spectacle of holy rollers, deviants
and the genetically perfected glory seekers
had them lined up for city blocks.
Oh, it's hard to care about truth's demise when the circus comes to town.

Vicki Whicker

Stagger Stumble

I just want to know if you're in or out
I guess by your non-answer you are in
Or you are out but don't want to tell me
Because you live like a terrorist
In this paper cut scream dashboard glass shatter stagger stumble
Last night at the blue white neon beer bar
Dance skinny and hold up your old jeans bar
Nod your head to the honky tonk beat and
        hope-that-your-life-isn't-over-yet bar
Despair-is-my-stringy-blonde-first-name bar
With a capital D
Lest you forget
Naked as lima beans we were a pair
Your hair when done with your pretty head was in my sink
Your wet towel next to mine tooth brush double squeeze not the midlife inhale
Go ahead, pretend you don't see me when you walk in the door
Pretend that I don't see you in the car outside my house with eyes low as
        the moon
That you don't love me like you did before
How did I get so lucky, you asked me
Love of my life, that was me last night
Singing with the band

Laura Caputo

Relative Concrete

If once the world could stand on its own
Open or closed—no matter
Then and only then would salvation be necessary
And if that is how the world might be
Then I will pray to You, Buddha, Jesus, Mohammad, Apollo, Aphrodite
Consider this my prayer
And if I believe what's inside of me is exactly what is outside
Wave "hello" to the scientists and walk on by, too
I need no saving, understanding would be nice, but I've given up on that
Given up on many things tonight
Tomorrow morning I will find reason
By afternoon chaos will ensue
Entropy proven
Order solidified
And on the way home, stop off at the gym for some expansion and contraction
"Home is where the heart is"
Home is what I'd like to find
Saw my heart on a monitor before
. . . heard it, too
Didn't feel like home but, boy, was it mesmerizing
Inside outside pause repeat
What if I close my eyes,
lost all of it tomorrow,
then what
What about that salvation I talked about before
Salvation from what, I ask
Confusion, a bad deed, a harsh experience, a challenging world
the end, the beginning
no! worse! the middle
If I stand over here you are nothing to me
And if I turn just half way round, you are I
A mirror image opposite and still whole
Backwards and still breathing
Art, politics, philosophy, religion, science
Bow down
Bow down

Bow down one more time
And you will find the answer
Spin to the left
Spin to the right
Go to a football game
And fight fight fight
The answer to knowing
The answer to not
The answer to thinking you do
The answer, the answer, the theory, the faith, the faithless
Culminate to this I don't know
And I know everything
Open for business
Closed for construction
Answer me this, O, scientists, philosophers, priests, animals, and gods
Where can I get a good slice of pizza in town?

Tim Giblin

Oaxaca, May 2006

I went back to see the girl last night that worked at the cafe by the truck stop. She smiled some more, I brought a phrase book, and read some sentences to her that I thought were appropriate, and then we laughed and I read some more, silly things about dancing and food. I stood in the kitchen, a brickback house with a concrete sink, where her friend cut shrimp in a bucket, and I begged for a kiss, and she and her friends laughed and giggled, but whenever I put a hand out to touch her she smacked it down. I slept in the van, on the side of the road, because I was scared to drive the curvy roads at night. I woke up at 6:00 and she was working, sweeping the dirt, and hosing down the road with water, and the trucks were idling, and the sun was coming up, and I left without saying goodbye. I saw her face in the passenger window as I pulled away; she had stopped sweeping and she just stood there looking at my van, and me.

Vicki Whicker

Poast Toastee

Inspired by her everyday life
Motivated by memory
She became a pillar of Himalayan salt
She begat the sun begat the moon
She burned Sodom and Gomorrah
Parted the ruby sea
Built an ark for everything
Fed the crowds crusty French bread
Multiplied the paisley fishes
The insult stuck in his eye and taped the lash with glue
No woman could do this
Have a house in the Palisades, a kid, a dog, a cat and a yard
He strung the web in the corner
He lipped her seeds of miniature
He wedged her into a green bottle
She wept
A deep rich red tinged with purple
Until her garden filled with crimson butterflies
Until he was lost in Ripple
Until he drowned in Burgundy

Leslie Berliant

Waiting for the Light

Inspired by her everyday life
of more of the same and the same and the same
ad infinitum, ad nauseum (add them all together and it's still a blank canvas),
she walked to the edge and looked down.
He sprawled out on his back, head at her heels
and said "Let me show you how I catch"
and had her bend backwards to reach his hands,
her body forming a bridge to nowhere special.
She hesitated for a moment.
The insult stuck in his eye and taped the lash with glue.
He came inside her anyway.
Afterwards she cried
from death and salt and the smell of someone so honest on her skin.
Two sets of eyes, hollow and terminal.
Two sets of forever good-byes.
Still he stayed,
his heart as open as her legs,
talking her through the seaweed and mollusk shells pulling her under.
He whispered in her ear promises of foreign lands and lost treasures
and waited with her for some light.

Julia Soto Frazer

Rocket Opossum

Inspired by her everyday life
or ordinary
or everyday
she couldn't decide . . .
she just knew she was tired
of using her inside voice while he
yawned and shouted and roared
loud alley shots of blustering smack.

Typical.

The insult stuck in his eye and taped the lash with glue.
Now she would have to tend him,
blink for him,
canary for him
in his scary coal mine of bruises
and sorrow and poem-hating reveries
while the edges of the furniture
pressed deeper into the carpet
and the plant tips crisped brown.

She waited and squirreled little rosehips of
delicious velvet drizzle for later.

Josh Rose

It used to be that whenever

It used to be that whenever I thought of you
Although now rot down in a gun hazed stocking mask
Bravely, fondly and bathed in the milky fuzz light of virginity
Pronounced with just the slight hint of lisp left over from childhood
With legs too young to touch
Mexico flirtations and all
It was all I could do to keep myself
From calling you back to a place we could neither live in
Nor have the appetite to visit
At the time, we were hungry
At the moment we were insane
We did things explored things touched things
We had no right to touch
Wrote things said things abused things
We never knew we would
And now you
With your baby in Texas
Me with mine half the time
I hardly ever think of you anymore
And when I do the smell of gun sulfur pulls me back.

Tim Giblin

Nicaragua, May 2006

I watch the kid pass his short board to a brown shadow on top of the chicken bus and the black plume of crow feathers bang a diesel drum as he splits. I wonder how much more I can take, how many more nights I can beat back this central belt of connective tissue between California and Panama. The sea is back like an angry woman claiming her due, and the soot sand makes a fine burial cloth for me. The children cry for dark brown kids that disappear into the whitewater. A cliff bilges and I am gone, gone again deep into the earth, gone again, a dot on the horizon, gone again lost in a serial mission. Gone quietly into the swell.

Laura Caputo

One of Those Days

I am sick and tired.
I am sick and tired.
I am sick and tired
of all of the noises on the street
in my head all around me.
I can't do this anymore, I
can't live like this.
I need to move away far away.
You know what I mean,
somewhere, not here . . .
like Mars or Venus . . .
as uninhabitable as this nasty place is.
I mean
have you seen the sky
have you looked up at the sun . . .
have you bothered to check out the dirty rotten mountains.
All of this is yuck,
I mean really yuck.
I can't believe it is easy for some to breathe
while I waste away
in dark bloody fat fuck land
where the grass is nothing but straw
and I'm no cow.
I don't think I am . . .
I don't look like anyone else
that's for sure,
but I'm really not a cow.
Somewhere but here I said.
Did you hear that part that he said
about butterflies
needing time in their cocoon,
needing the dark and the moist inside.
I already did dark and moist . . .
9 months
13 days
and 14 hours

of dark moist
and way uncomfortable coming out.
Good god, ha!
Good god . . .
what about bad god . . .
what about the training wheels
that were supposed to save me from the fall . . .
what about the direct result of 52 years and 48 days.

Julia Soto Frazer

Blam Cantankerous

He pushed me against the wall. Not in a bad way. In a make-out way. The wall was cold through my dress, my little black dress, the kind you wear in Paris. The wallpaper was faded in a charmingly French way and I suddenly thought the word *bourgeois* and wondered if I was one. I also wondered if this was being secretly filmed and would show up on an Internet site of hotel hallway sex—the too-bright light would be perfect. I smelled sweet, like crème brûlée. A bed creaked in a room somewhere. It was 3:00 A.M. and I wasn't supposed to be doing this. "I'm not going to sleep with you," I said, and blam cantankerous bully ram crepe paper, crepe paper, crepe paper, crepe.

So. This is what you've become—a cheating whore, a two-timing shrewish cunt-opening beast. If you aren't supposed to be doing this, then why are you, you butter-smothered lardass? That dress doesn't fit you. Christ in a handbasket! Eiffel Towers couldn't drag you away from this night and the drunken mad hatteredness of that cobbled cab ride.

I swallowed my tongue and couldn't give directions. I motioned to my date, pointing to my mouth and the now empty hole. "Rue Bouillabaisse," he said, and as the cab drove on, I felt my tongue slipping through the chortled areas of my esophagus, places where I had laughed too hard and too inappropriately. The cab stopped. We got out. My date walked beside me, chain dragging—bright blue to match his suit. On the boulevard, others were walking. Some men's chains were thick and wide, others thin and heavy. One's sang "Allons enfants de la Patrie," whatever that meant. I didn't understand any of it, but these men were French and style was mother's milk to them, like cognac and popes' wine in cellars that stretched for miles under catacombs where Jesus lived in his missing years, drunk on Brie and sniffing coke.

I followed him over the embankment to the edge of the Seine. His chain provided him with a nice drag whereas I was slipping. I turned sideways so my feet would find lengthwise purchase. *Merde!* I said. But it came out, Ungh! on account of the missing tongue. Ungh! I said again, and no one, including him, helped me. (I had heard the French were rude.) We made it to the edge of the river. He reached into the bucket of strawberries the government provided and handed me one. I opened my palm, muddy and scratched. "Eat," he said. Ungh! I said, putting it in my mouth and making a pulpy, gritty mash of it. It was a lovely strawberry. Really it was.

But, Satan in an Easter Egg! Didn't your mother teach you not to take sweets from strangers? Think, for God's sake! I know that a strawberry is not technically a sweet, but it is sweet and sweetness delivers. Ineffectual men will do that, won't they? They'll make you stray, they'll make you cover the waterfront, they'll make you go to France in a black dress the shape of a woman you have never met but who occupies you like Napoleon.

3:01 A.M. I put my hand on the doorknob and turned to watch his descent. He was stalled on the stairs, his hand on the banister, his body twisted downwards, his head swiveled upwards. Picasso painted like this: impossible contortions, limbs piled on limbs, women missing tongues and the world a little more than real. A large, white, plywood box was at the top of the stairwell; I supposed that's where he'd sat me when he'd pushed his body between my legs, when my stocking had snagged, when I was at my most desirable. The elevator clunked and lifted from the floor below. My dress felt tight around my middle and my crème brûlée aroma had soured. "I had a lovely time," I said.

I stepped into my room and shut the door.

I reviewed the evening: I wasn't supposed to have done what I had done, I probably was a "bourgeois" and I smelled burnt toast. Breakfast, already?

Not for me. The bed looked deliciously lumpy and I wanted to jump in. But, not yet. I needed to feel one more second go by.

There it went.

Alan Berman

The Script

Did you know I was once
but I'm not anymore.
I'm not, not now. I was
once, just once. Now that's over.
I repeat myself because that's how it works:
there's a less-simple way of explaining it
that I could have offered when I was,
but it's too late for that, I can't tell you how late.
Just accept it, I told myself when they first approached me about it.
They wanted all of it, but in the end, I agreed to sell them four years
and I didn't tell them I was thinking with all my heart *dog* years,
which is a bargain if you ask me; I mean, it's a lifetime for some
dogs, for some people I've heard about. But they weren't clairvoyant,
so the deal stuck at four regular years. I needed a break and would
have let them have four dog years' worth if they could have read my mind.
But they must now know what I'm missing—it turns out that I
haven't been this whole time, that is, since they came to me,
and not being is not what I expected it would be, but probably
just what they wanted. I got the worst side of the deal and
I cannot tell anyone who is.

Elaine Mintzer
Do You Want Your Brain to Hurt Now or Later?
13 LOS ANGELES POETS
CHAOS and DANCING STARS
Jean Katz
poems
BREAKING DOWN THE SURFACE OF THE WORLD

www.ingramcontent.com/pod-product-compliance
Lightning Source LLC
Chambersburg PA
CBHW020918090426
42736CB00008B/693

9780941017824